Books by Charles M. Schulz

Peanuts
More Peanuts
Good Grief, More Peanuts!
Good Ol' Charlie Brown
Snoopy
You're Out of Your Mind, Charlie Brown!
But We Love You, Charlie Brown
Peanuts Revisited
Go Fly a Kite, Charlie Brown
Peanuts Every Sunday
It's a Dog's Life, Charlie Brown
You Can't Win, Charlie Brown
Snoopy, Come Home
You Can Do It, Charlie Brown
We're Right Behind You, Charlie Brown
As You Like It, Charlie Brown
Sunday's Fun Day, Charlie Brown
You Need Help, Charlie Brown
Snoopy and the Red Baron
The Unsinkable Charlie Brown
You'll Flip, Charlie Brown
You're Something Else, Charlie Brown
Peanuts Treasury
You're You, Charlie Brown
You've Had It, Charlie Brown
Snoopy and His Sopwith Camel
A Boy Named Charlie Brown
You're Out of Sight, Charlie Brown
Peanuts Classics
You've Come a Long Way, Charlie Brown
Snoopy and "It Was a Dark and Stormy Night"
"Ha Ha, Herman," Charlie Brown

PEANUTS®

By CHARLES M. SCHULZ

HOLT, RINEHART AND WINSTON
NEW YORK · CHICAGO · SAN FRANCISCO

RATS! HE CAN EVEN HEAR ME LAPPING AN ICE-CREAM CONE!!

SCHULZ

IT'S NO USE...I JUST CAN'T DO IT...

WHAT'S THE MATTER, CHARLIE BROWN? YOU LOOK DISCOURAGED

I WANTED TO BUILD MYSELF A WORKBENCH.....

BUT I DON'T HAVE A WORKBENCH TO BUILD IT ON!!

SCHULZ

KNOCK! KNOCK!

TRICKS OR TREATS... MONEY OR EATS!

WHAT?!

GET OUT OF HERE!!! HALLOWEEN WAS YESTERDAY!

I'M STILL HUNGRY!

SLAM!

SCHULZ

IF I CAN SAVE TWO-THOUSAND OF THESE BOX TOPS, I GET A TRICYCLE!

I'VE GOT IT ALL FIGURED OUT...I EAT ABOUT ONE BOX OF THIS STUFF EVERY WEEK...

THAT MEANS I'LL HAVE ENOUGH BOX TOPS BY THE TIME I'M FORTY!

BUT WHAT AM I GOING TO DO WITH A TRICYCLE WHEN I'M FORTY YEARS OLD?

SCHULZ